PRESENTED TO

....

FROM

....

DATE

....

DADS &
DAUGHTERS

*Timeless wisdom and
reflections on teaching, guiding,
and loving your daughter—
her whole life long*

DR. JAMES DOBSON

TYNDALE
MOMENTUM™

*The nonfiction imprint of
Tyndale House Publishers, Inc.*

Visit Tyndale online at www.tyndale.com.

Visit Tyndale Momentum online at www.tyndalemomentum.com.

TYNDALE, Tyndale Momentum, and Tyndale's quill logo are registered trademarks of Tyndale House Publishers, Inc. The Tyndale Momentum logo is a trademark of Tyndale House Publishers, Inc. Tyndale Momentum is the nonfiction imprint of Tyndale House Publishers, Inc., Carol Stream, Illinois.

Dads and Daughters

Copyright © 2013 by James C. Dobson. All rights reserved.

Cover photograph copyright © Blend Images/Veer. All rights reserved.

Author photograph copyright © 2004 by Harry Langdon. All rights reserved.

Literary development and design: Koechel Peterson & Associates, Inc., Minneapolis, Minnesota.

Interior and back cover photographs are the property of their respective copyright owners and © Thinkstock.com. All rights reserved.

This book has been adapted from *Bringing Up Girls: Practical Advice and Encouragement for Those Shaping the Next Generation of Women,* copyright © 2010 by James C. Dobson. Published by Tyndale House Publishers.

All Scripture quotations, unless otherwise indicated, are taken from the Holy Bible, *New International Version,*® *NIV.*® Copyright © 1973, 1978, 1984 by Biblica, Inc.® Used by permission. All rights reserved worldwide.

Scripture quotations marked KJV are taken from the *Holy Bible,* King James Version.

For information about special discounts for bulk purchases, please contact Tyndale House Publishers at csresponse@tyndale.com, or call 1-800-323-9400.

ISBN 978-1-4143-8822-9

Printed in China

22   21   20   19   18   17
7   6   5   4   3   2

CONTENTS

From One Dad's Heart to Another • 6

What It Means to Be a Dad • 10

Dads Hold the Keys • 14

She Urgently Needs You • 18

Fight for Your Daughter • 22

Every Little Girl • 26

A Place in Your Heart • 30

The Power of Conversation • 34

The Art of Conversation • 38

When the Fireworks Begin • 44

When the Sky Seems to Be Falling • 50

The Power of Touch • 56

Knock Down Barriers, Build Bridges • 60

Give the Love Only You Can Give • 64

Why Dads Matter • 68

Does She Know She's Your Princess? • 72

Be There for Her • 76

Discipline with Love and Respect • 80

Win the Battle of Wills • 88

Friends and Bullies • 92

Your Most Significant Responsibility • 98

Teach Your Daughter Well • 102

Give Her the Divine Source of Wisdom • 106

The Power of Prayer • 110

She Is Worth the Sacrifice • 114

Every Dad Has Some Regrets • 118

Remember, Dads • 122

Endnotes • 126

From One Dad's Heart
TO ANOTHER

The passion I feel for the subject at hand is related to the daughter who still calls me Dad. Danae is grown now, but I love her like I did when we were first introduced in the delivery room. Something electric occurred between us on that mystical night, and it endures today. I thank God for the privilege of being the father of this remarkable woman!

Being a father and a type A personality myself, I look back on my parenting experiences and recall instances where I could have done a better job. I wish I could relive some of those busy days at a slower pace. Unfortunately, none of us is allowed do-overs or mulligans. When our record is finally in the books, not a word or a deed can be altered.

Would it be self-serving to tell you that I also did some things right during my early days as a father, and that the memories of some very special times with my kids rank at the top of my list of accomplishments today? Among my favorites are recollections of Danae when she was five years old. We used to take bike trips together to a nearby park on Saturday mornings and play in a sandbox with shovels and buckets. I taught her to build sand castles, explained what a moat and a drawbridge were, and talked about anything else that seemed to interest her. Then we would go to a nearby taco stand and have lunch before riding home. On the way back, we listened every week to a favorite recording of Rodgers and Hammerstein's *Cinderella* on a small Craig recorder, and we sang the songs together. Danae loved those outings, and she can tell you in detail about them today. And guess what? I loved them too.

> *From where I sit today, I can say that nothing, and I mean nothing, from that era turned out to be more significant than the hours I spent with my little family. The relationships we enjoy today were nurtured during those years when it would have been very easy for me to chase every professional prize and ignore what mattered most at home.*

Some years ago I asked our radio listeners to call our organization and record a message for their dads. More than six hundred people participated, and not one caller focused on what their father did professionally. None of them said, "Thanks, Dad, for earning a lot of money" or "Thanks for the big house you provided for us." Instead, caller after caller said, *"Thanks, Dad, for loving me and for being there for me."* Some said with strong emotion, *"Thank you for letting me interrupt you, even when you were busy."* Nearly all of the calls coming from women mentioned *the presence of tenderness* in the relationship.

I address this specifically to dads who are still raising daughters and want to respond to the desires of their little hearts. My advice is also relevant to fathers whose daughters are grown. The woman who used to be "Dad's little princess" may still long for what she didn't receive when she was young. Even though these fathers can no longer play in the sandbox with their five-year-olds, it is never too late for them to say,

You are precious to me.

What I am sharing with you has become my obsession. I get a lump in my throat when I think of our precious kids who know so little about life, and I worry about how we can protect their innocence and preserve the joys of childhood.

That is our task as dads. So get a cup of hot coffee or put on a kettle of tea, settle down in a comfortable chair, and let's talk together.

What It Means
TO BE A DAD

Fathers inevitably change the course of their daughters'
lives—and can even save them. From the moment you
set eyes on her wet-from-the-womb body until she
leaves your home, the clock starts ticking. It's the clock
that times your hours with her, your opportunities to
influence her, to shape her character, and to help her
find herself—and to enjoy living. [1]

Dr. Meg Meeker

Pediatrician Meg Meeker has written a wonderful book entitled *Strong Fathers, Strong Daughters*, in which she writes brilliantly about the way girls are made as well as the difference fathers make in their daughters' lives. The influence that dads wield for good or harm in their daughters' lives touches every dimension of life.

Parents have a fundamental responsibility of not simply overseeing the growth and development of their girls (and boys) but of raising them purposely—building into them certain qualities and traits of character. Wise King Solomon addressed that obligation more than 2,900 years ago when he wrote, "Train up a child in the way he should go: and when he is old, he will not depart from it" (Proverbs 22:6, KJV). The apostle Paul added another dimension when he said, "Fathers, do not exasperate your children; instead, bring them up in the training and instruction of the Lord" (Ephesians 6:4).

As a father, think for a moment about the implications of these Scriptures.

> *First and foremost, they mean a child*
> *should be taught to revere God and His*
> *Son, Jesus Christ, and to understand the*
> *spiritual dimension of life.*

But they instruct us to do more than that. Children are a gift from God, and we are stewards of their welfare. Training up our daughters in this sense means to:

- *Help them to navigate the cultural minefields that lie in their paths.*
- *Teach them eternal values, talents, and perspectives.*
- *Instill within them an appreciation for truthfulness, trustworthiness, self-discipline, self-control, generosity, and sweetness of spirit.*
- *Teach them modesty, morality, and manners.*
- *Teach them to work and learn and think.*

That is just the beginning, which is why parenthood is such a daunting responsibility, requiring careful forethought and planning.

As fathers, how can we allow ourselves to get so busy with the cares of life that we neglect our vulnerable little girls and leave them unprotected from evil influences? How can we fail to give them the love and attention they crave? And how can we send them into a dangerous world without laying a secure foundation to hold them steady? No other priority comes close to this responsibility to raise our children, as Solomon said, in the way they should go.

Children are a gift from God,
and we are stewards of their welfare.

Dads
HOLD THE KEYS

A father holds the keys
to his daughter's feminine identity,
her sense of self-worth,
and her future relationships.

A dad's affirmation, or the lack thereof,
will play a role in every aspect of her life,
even influencing her choice
of a marital partner.

There is a place in the female soul reserved for Daddy, or a daddy figure, that will always yearn for affirmation. Not every girl or woman is the same, of course, but almost every girl desires a close bond with this most significant man in her life. She will adore him if he loves and protects her and if she finds safety and warmth in his arms. She will feel that way throughout life unless he disappoints her. She will tend to see all men through the lens of that relationship. If he rejects and ignores her, or worse, if he abuses and abandons her, the yearning within her becomes more intense, though it is often tainted with resentment and anger.

Let me make another thing clear: mothers cannot fill this particular empty space. They can and must meet similar needs for love and adoration, and in fact they do occupy their own real estate in a daughter's heart. A girl without a mother's love is a sad spectacle indeed, and I would not minimize the maternal role in any regard. But *moms can't be dads,* and *dads can't be moms.*

Why do girls and women have such intense needs for affirmation from their fathers, and why does the hurt caused by abandonment or rejection often reverberate for a lifetime? A primary reason for this inner ache is because a daughter's sense of self-worth and confidence is linked directly to her relationship with her dad.[2] What he thinks about her and how he expresses his affection is a central source of her perceived value as a human being. It also affects her femininity and teaches her how to relate to boys and men.

If you wonder whether you hold the keys to your daughter's life, consider Dr. Meg Meeker's insightful perspective.

> I have watched daughters talk to fathers.
> When you come into the room, they change.
> Everything about them changes: their eyes,
> their mouths, their gestures, their body
> language. Daughters are never lukewarm
> in the presence of their fathers. They might
> take their mothers for granted, but not you.
> They light up—or they cry. They watch you
> intensely. They hang on your words. They
> hope for your attention, and they wait for it in
> frustration—or in despair. They need a gesture
> of approval, a nod of encouragement, or even
> simple eye contact to let them know you care
> and are willing to help.[3]
>
> Dr. Meg Meeker

There is a place in the female soul
reserved for Daddy that will always
yearn for affirmation.

She Urgently NEEDS YOU

F athers know intuitively that their boys require special attention, discipline, and leadership, but *they are often unaware of how urgently their daughters also need them.* Some dads apparently see this yearning for affirmation among their girls as the exclusive responsibility of mothers. Raising daughters is seen as "women's work." Thus, the girls are often overlooked or largely ignored. However,

Girls need their dads as much as boys do,
and in some cases, even more.
Furthermore, when girls are deprived
of the needed affirmation,
an inner longing occurs that may continue
for the rest of their lives.

These haunting words from a woman in her late thirties still echo in my mind today:

> *Hi, this is Kathy from Georgia, with a letter for my daddy. I don't know where things went wrong, when the pain, prescriptions, and alcohol began. I was just a kid. You tried to never let me down, Daddy, but many times you did. Daddy, in 1978, always and still, I was thinking of you as Father's Day approached. I searched for just the right card for you, my darling daddy, and mailed it late. But Daddy, all day long your phone was busy. You died alone on the floor, beside your upturned phone, on Father's Day. When I got to Portland, my card was still in your mailbox. You never knew, Daddy. I was too late. God, help*

me always to remember that late is better than
never, but it's not good enough. Daddy, you died
without experiencing my care and my love on
Father's Day.

Even though decades had passed since the painful experience of her childhood, this woman continued to grieve for her absentee father. Her "darling daddy" was never there for her. It didn't have to be this way.

Your daughter needs you more than you can imagine. If you still wonder, consider these words from a female college student whom I interviewed:

No matter how much your mom affirms you as
a child, she can't compensate fully if something
is missing in your relationship with your dad.
Even if you have a full-time mom when you are
growing up, you still need the validation of your
dad. When he doesn't provide it, your entire life
is affected and even the way you see things is
different. That has happened to me.

Girls need their dads as much as boys do, and in some cases, even more.

Fight for Your
DAUGHTER

Today's girls, including your daughter, are being enticed to grow up too fast and are encountering challenges for which they are totally unprepared. Their turmoil is evident within an array of harmful behaviors, such as eating disorders and an obsession with extreme thinness. Although it has numerous and complex psychological causes, it is driven primarily by a fear of being fat, or even chubby, during the childhood and adolescent years. Never before have children been so preoccupied with the shapes of their bodies. And there are many other serious concerns for middle and high school students.

Helping to promote some of this dangerous and antisocial behavior is an array of "bad girls"—the pop icons, starlets, and American idols who have become role models for millions of girls. Although the in-crowd is constantly changing, their lifestyles help to warp this generation of young girls. How can awkward, newly minted teenagers with braces and acne measure up to these perceived standards of perfection?

This is the key that you need to understand as a father:

Our society is at war with good parents
who are trying desperately to protect their kids
from the harmful forces swirling around them.

With our children caught in this culture's crosshairs, we must fight back with all our resources. Heaven help our kids if fathers remain passive and disconnected. Our children desperately need us to guide their steps and set reasonable boundaries to protect them. You can fill the void that will otherwise send your daughters on a desperate search for nurturance and affirmation.

My father was a good man, but he was very passive, and I just wish he would have set a lot more boundaries and given me more critical input. That is what I missed most from him. Instead of worrying so much about hurting my feelings, I wish he had shown me that he had an opinion of what was right and wrong in my life. He was always trying to make sure that I was happy with our relationship, but I would rather that he would have been more forthright and said, 'You know, I don't think this guy is right for you. This is what I see.' I needed him to tell me that I mattered enough for him to guide me.

From a Female College Student

Your public school can't be counted on to protect your daughter.
Your church may be helpful, but even it is not enough.
You, however, can provide the care and guidance that is needed.

Every Little Girl

I discovered I didn't feel ... worthy of love, unless I was

accomplishing something. I suddenly realized I have

never felt I could be loved just for being.[4]

Oprah Winfrey

Oprah Winfrey was the most successful woman in television for more than twenty-five years. Millions of viewers tuned in to her talk show every day and have been influenced by what she has to say. She is also one of the wealthiest women in the world. This, however, is how she sees herself.

There is no end to the examples I could cite of admired, respected, and gorgeous women—from Chris Evert to Melissa Gilbert to Ava Gardner to Marilyn Monroe—who were never entirely comfortable in their own skin. I served as a school psychologist before moving into academia and saw evidence of this vulnerability in most of our female students. They didn't feel pretty enough or accepted by their peers. They just weren't valuable in their own eyes.

I have discovered that the phenomenon of low self-worth can be irrational and is not always linked to obvious causes. To some degree, it is "every woman." And it begins in childhood.

John and Stasi Eldredge described this nature in their book entitled *Captivating: Unveiling the Mystery of a Woman's Soul*. They wrote:

> *Every little girl . . .*
> *is asking one fundamental question. . . .*
> *Little girls want to know,*
>
> *"Am I lovely?"*
>
> *The twirling skirts, the dress up,*
> *the longing to be pretty and to be seen—*
> *that's what that's all about.*
>
> *We are seeking an answer to our Question. . . .*
>
> *We live haunted by that Question,*
> *yet unaware that it still needs an answer.*[5]

Perhaps you are asking, "Well, what can we as parents do about this 'unanswered question' within our daughters? How can we raise them to be confident women? Is there a way to preserve their softness and femininity while strengthening their sense of personhood too?"

I believe there are many approaches to instilling healthy self-worth in girls, but it begins within the security of a loving family. Specifically, it depends on a caring and affirming father. Moms are vital in countless ways too, but self-worth for girls hangs precariously on their relationship with their dads.

A Place in Your HEART

Work at building your daughter's self-concept
throughout her childhood.

Tell her she is pretty every chance you get.

Hug her.

Compliment her admirable traits.

Build her confidence by giving her
your time and attention.

Defend her when she is struggling.

And let her know that
she has a place in your heart
that is reserved only for her.
She will never forget it.

Childhood lasts for only a brief moment,
so give it priority while she is
passing before your eyes.
Watch your daughter carefully.
Think about what she is feeling,
and consider the influences she is under.
Then do what is best for her.

When my dad started showing me how much he loved me, I realized how much God loves me. I never felt worthy of love by anyone until my dad started showing it to me.

From a Female College Student

The Power of CONVERSATION

One of the cornerstones of human relationships

is embodied in a single word: conversation.

As you seek to understand your daughter, another major factor you must not overlook is that there is 15 percent more blood flowing in the female brain than in that of a male, and it is more likely to surge to both hemispheres.[6] When you talk to a girl, she is concentrating on what you say with both sides of her brain, whereas a boy is listening with predominately one side. This is why females typically like to process ideas before deciding or acting on them. It is also why women often agonize over routine decisions.

It is impossible to overstate the importance of talking in the lives of girls and women. Though estimates vary, it appears that males use about seven thousand words per day; and females, twenty thousand.[7] Women not only talk more, but their enjoyment in conversation is far more intense. Girls and women, more than boys and men, connect emotionally through spoken words. *Connecting through talking activates the pleasure centers of a girl's brain, providing a huge emotional reward for her.* It is why teen girls are obsessed with text messaging and computer chat rooms. It also explains why one of the most common sources of disappointment women express about married life is that the guys won't talk to them. When communication breaks down between them and people they love, females are often wounded and frustrated.

*Females of all ages
tend to interpret masculine silence
as evidence of rejection.
Girls often feel abandoned by fathers
who won't engage them verbally.*

Based on this understanding, the best thing dads can do to connect with their daughters is to talk to them about whatever is of interest. Little and not-so-little girls need to talk, especially about what they are feeling. Ask questions and then listen carefully to what is said in return. This interaction helps to produce the affirmation she needs. Meaningful and affectionate dialogue with a daughter is evidence that she is worthy, secure, and loved. Those beneficial effects can be achieved so easily through simple, genuine conversation.

Let me speak directly to the busy dad who is too exhausted at the end of the day to get your daughter talking, either at the dinner table or in those intimate few minutes before bedtime: you may be making a serious mistake. You need to know what she is thinking, and she needs the pleasure of telling you about it. It is imperative that you tune in. There will come a time when she will be talking primarily to her peers, and the missed opportunities for understanding and intimacy today will be costly down the road.

Engage your daughter in activities that encourage conversation, including eating together as a family, playing table games, inviting friends with kids to dinner, cooking together, building things, adopting a lovable dog or cat, cultivating mutual interests, or learning a sport such as skiing or tennis as a family.

Remember how your daughter is made,
and seek invitations into her private world.
You won't regret it.

The Art of CONVERSATION

The hardest job kids face today

is learning good manners

without seeing any.[8]

Fred Astaire

In our twenty-first century culture, young girls are often allowed, and even encouraged, to be brash, rude, crude, profane, immodest, immoral, loud, and aggressive. As challenging as it is, parents are responsible to teach their daughters the enduring principles of right and wrong as well as social graces and manners of civility that help them become ladies. That instruction ranges from something as basic as learning to say thank you and please and techniques of personal grooming, hygiene, and nutrition to more advanced instructions about being gracious hosts, how to formally introduce parents or friends to each other, how to take turns talking in a group, and how to make eye contact.

As a father, one of the ways you can help your children significantly is to help them learn the art of conversation, which is becoming a lost skill in these days of text messaging. I offer this as a technique that I have found to be very effective.

It begins by facing your daughter about six feet away and telling her that you are going to play a game together. Then call attention to the tennis ball you are holding, which you proceed to bounce in her direction. After she catches the ball, stand there looking at each other for a moment before saying, "It isn't much fun if you hold the ball, is it? Why don't you throw it back?" Your daughter will probably return the ball rather quickly. Stand motionless for few seconds, and then say, "Okay, I'm sending it back to you now." She will be curious about what is going on. Then sit down together and describe the meaning of the game. Tell her that talking together is a game called conversation, and it only works if the "ball" is thrown back. If a person bounces a question to you and you hold it, the game ends. Neither you nor your partner has any fun. But if you throw it back, you are playing the game properly.

Follow up by saying, "Suppose I ask, 'Did you like the book you have been reading?' I have thrown the ball to you. If you simply reply, 'Yes,' you have caught and held the ball. But if you say, 'The book was very interesting. I like reading about animals,' you have thrown the ball back."

Then tell your daughter, "I can keep our conversation going by asking, 'What kind of animals interest you most?' If you say, 'Dogs,' you have held the ball again. But if you tell me, 'I like dogs because they are warm and cuddly,' the ball has been bounced back to me. The idea is to keep the game going until the two of us are finished talking."

Kids usually catch on to this game quickly. Afterward, you can build on the concept by commenting on interchanges that occur with friends and adults. For example, you might ask your daughter, "Did you hear Mrs. Smith ask you this afternoon what kind of food you liked? She was starting a conversation with you, but you just said, 'Hamburgers.' Do you think you threw the ball back to her?"

The child may acknowledge that she held it. Then the two of you can discuss what could have been done differently. Suggest, perhaps, that the question could have been tossed back by saying, "I like the hamburgers my mother makes."

Mrs. Smith might then have asked, "What makes them so good?"

"That," you tell the youngster, "is another example of a conversation. Let's practice 'throwing the ball' to each other. Now, start one with me."

When you teach your children the art of conversation, you help them develop confidence and poise. A girl who has been trained properly in her conversation skills as well as manners is never completely knocked off balance when she is in an unfamiliar circumstance. She knows what is expected of her and how to deal with it. Her sense of self-worth is reinforced by the way adults react to her charm, poise, and grace. If you want to give your daughter a head start in life and help her compete socially, this is a great place to begin.

> *Teaching manners to girls is about helping them to become young ladies in a not-very-civil world. I assure you that MTV and an increasingly crude culture will do everything possible to carry your daughter downstream toward that which is boorish and uncouth. You can help her paddle upstream.*

The art of conversation is becoming a lost skill in these days of text messaging.

When the
FIREWORKS BEGIN

strogen and other hormones wire a young girl's brain
for femininity and prepare it for all that will come with
the onset of puberty. Typically between the ages of twelve
and thirteen, the girl enters a period of intense physical,
emotional, and neurological transformation that is genetically
controlled, and the changes that occur will affect the rest of
her life. The more you understand about this challenging
phase of her growing up years, the better equipped you will
be to help her through it.

In a nutshell, when the time is right, hormones are secreted into the girl's bloodstream that flow to the ovaries and cause the production of massive amounts of estrogen. Thus, her brain is marinated for a second time in this female hormone, which begins to spur maturation and sexual development. Three other primary hormones are involved in puberty: progesterone, testosterone, and growth hormones.[9] When they work in concert, it is like fireworks on the Fourth of July.

Within her, a delicate feedback mechanism comes into play that fine-tunes the constantly fluctuating hormones in a specified fashion, thereby allowing the miracle of ovulation and, as some would say, the curse of menstruation. These elevated levels also influence a multitude of functions and emotions, including anger, sorrow, joy, memory, aggression, thirst, appetite, weight, fat distribution, the development of secondary sex characteristics such as pubic hair, and higher intellectual functioning. In short, they bring about a makeover of the body and the personality. It all begins happening very quickly. So brace yourself!

You should understand that the hormonal barrage that initiates puberty is highly traumatic to the female brain, and it can throw a girl into complete disequilibrium until she begins to adjust to it.[10] This is why you must take the time to understand what she is going through. From pubescence through adolescence, there will be recurring times of moodiness, anxiety, anger, self-pity, and depression. There will also be periods of giddiness, glee, elation, and happiness. Emotions are on a roller coaster from the peak to the valley, and from one day—or one hour—to the next. The entire family sometimes hangs on for dear life until things start to settle down. For some girls, the return to equilibrium can take five years or longer.

What does a girl need from her parents when everything has gone topsy-turvy? The answer, in a word, is *more attachment, not less.* Even when she is most unlovable, she needs love and connectedness from her mother, but also from her father. She needs them to be as calm, mature, and parental as possible. There is no room in their relationship for an out-of-control, screaming, confused, and scared adult. A voice of reason is desperately needed, even with a child who has become entirely unreasonable. I know this is difficult advice to receive or implement because a pubescent girl can be absolutely maddening. Strange impulses are urging them to do things that make no sense to a rational mind, and many of them can't help responding the way they do.

Fathers are extremely important in the midst of this chaos. If their temperaments allow, they can be the "voice of reason" to which I referred. Fathers can help interpret motives, mitigate harsh words, and soothe hurt feelings across the generational gap. But if Dad also starts to go berserk, it's Katie bar the door.

The surprising thing is that at the same time puberty is causing girls to pull away from the people they love, other forces inside them are creating an inexplicable longing for connectedness.

Just as estrogen drives the need for intimacy in infancy, it has the same effect in puberty and adolescence, only this time it is even more intense. The desire for social bonding, especially with peers, causes great vulnerability. This is why adolescents travel in packs. It is to protect themselves. *The most paralyzing fear for a girl in these years is the prospect of being left out, rejected, criticized, or humiliated.* Even the most minor criticism from parents can produce a tsunami of tears and retribution. Overreaction becomes an everyday event. Heaven help the mom or dad who tries to convince a sobbing girl that "it's no big deal." They are wrong. Everything is a big deal.

To be wounded by a boy can seem like a fate worse than death to a vulnerable girl. That is because *during puberty and adolescence, the most urgent biological impulse is to be perceived as sexually desirable.* It explains why girls spend hours in front of mirrors, examining, fretting, preening, rearranging, enhancing, wishing, and caking on makeup. Most do not like what they see. Looking back at them are images of braces, acne, misshapen noses, protruding ears, freckles, or "impossible" hair.

As parents, your job is to understand these pressures and then to help your daughter cope as much as possible.

When the Sky Seems TO BE FALLING

A nother area of your daughter's life requires your basic understanding—her monthly cycle and how it influences her mind and body. It is impossible to comprehend how a teen girl feels about herself, about her family, about her life, and about her peers without considering the impact of her cycle and the fluctuating hormones that drive it. While every woman is different, this is the way the system usually works.

During the first week after a menstrual period, estrogen levels are on the rise, producing surging amounts of energy, ambition, and optimism. Her world looks bright, and her mood is upbeat. During the second week, estrogen reaches its peak and then levels off. A pubescent or adolescent girl in this phase remains energetic, but she paces herself more moderately. She is still confident, creative, and, depending on other circumstances, might be euphoric. It takes a great deal to upset or worry her.

About midcycle, during the start of the third week, a young woman experiences ovulation and her time of fertility. Estrogen levels then rebound for a few days. These developments coincide with her peak of sexual desire. It is also during this week that she feels deep devotion, affection, and closeness for the boy or man she loves. We can say with a smile that there is a God-designed "conspiracy" at work here to assure the propagation of the human race. You and I would not have existed without it.

Then estrogen, progesterone, and endorphin levels plummet in the fourth week. As a result, a girl's mood darkens and she becomes more "within herself." These hormonal changes are very toxic to the brain and can create depression and foreboding, low self-esteem, hypersensitivity, sadness, and anger. Also, she typically feels unloved and insecure. She may sense she is "in a fog" and may walk into a room and not remember why she is there. Even her performance in school can be affected. Alas, she is experiencing the symptoms known around the world as premenstrual syndrome. It is followed in about three days by a period, with its cramping, bloating, and malaise. And so ends the four-week cycle. It is followed quickly by a surge of estrogen and the return of good times.

> *When she is wailing and complaining*
> *and despairing over this or that, she needs*
> *attachment. She needs comfort and love. And*
> *she needs a few more days to move on past the*
> *blues. Sounds easy, right? It ain't.*

As if that isn't challenging enough, there is another hormonal secretion that is almost mischievous in its influence. It is oxytocin, which is nicknamed "the cuddle hormone,"[11] and you can figure out where it leads. When a girl gets to know a guy and feels safe with him, her oxytocin levels rise, giving her a rush of hope, trust, optimism, confidence, and a feeling that all her needs will be met.[12] She may start to fall in love with him, or something that feels like love for a while, but not because he is the perfect human being. He is perceived as the perfect human being because she starts to feel like it. Hugging and snuggling cause oxytocin levels to surge, which leads to more hugging and snuggling. Talk about a tender trap!

Remember, our biochemistry is designed to guarantee the continuation of the human race, with hormones, receptor sites, brain wiring, and neurotransmitters effectively carrying impulses from cell to cell. Oxytocin is a powerful component of that apparatus. Dr. Brizendine says, "From an experiment on hugging, we also know that oxytocin is naturally released in the brain after a twenty-second hug from a partner—sealing the bond between huggers and triggering the brain's trust circuits. So don't let a guy hug you unless you plan to trust him."[13] Do you think you can help your daughter understand that hormone? No chance. You just have to hope her boyfriend doesn't know how it works.

What I have tried to share to this point is an understanding of what your pubescent daughter is experiencing and why—days of exhilaration and despair, falling madly in love over and over and over. Wise parents can shepherd their youngsters through these early experiences and make them fun and clean. Adult supervision is absolutely necessary, however, to keep a girl or boy from getting too far ahead of themselves and doing things that will be harmful for decades to come. They also need help in understanding what is happening inside and recognizing that the unstable emotions that come flooding over them at times are temporary.

Most of all, stay connected,
especially in the dark days
when the sky seems to be falling.
It usually isn't.

The Power of Touch

Touch is another point of connection that is essential to girls. Just like their mothers, our daughters need to be hugged regularly, perhaps every day. Hugging is easy to do when girls are young and they see their daddies as champions and best buddies. However, with the arrival of puberty and evidences of sexual maturation, fathers often feel uneasy and tend to avoid physical contact. Girls can read that discomfort with the accuracy of a laser.[14]

One girl gave me a textbook example of the way fathers often respond to their daughters during puberty and adolescence. She said,

> When I was going from a child to a woman—
> experiencing puberty—my dad just totally
> stepped back from me. It was as though he no
> longer knew how to relate to me. But it was a
> time when I desperately needed him in my life.

The awkwardness of this girl's father, I would guess, was related to her breast development and womanly appearance. Some fourteen- or fifteen-year-old girls already have the bodies of women, and their dads are not supposed to notice—but they do. A loving father is afraid he will touch her in the wrong place or otherwise offend her. So he tries to keep a discreet distance.

On the other side of the ledger, a girl who has wrestled with her father and hugged and kissed him throughout childhood can't possibly understand why he leans away now when she throws her arms around him. What makes the situation worse is that younger children in the family, both boys and girls, still snuggle up to Dad and tell him they love him. The budding teenager sees that affection and wants to cry over what she has lost.

The girl who observed her father stepping back from her quite naturally concluded that *"Daddy doesn't love me anymore."* That scenario has been enacted by millions of fathers and daughters around the world.

I want to say to all these dads emphatically that your pubescent and adolescent girls are going through a time of great insecurity. *They desperately need you now.* You are their protector and their source of stability. Your love now is critical to their ability to cope with the rejection, hurt, and fears that are coming at them from their peers. Hugs are needed now more than ever; a loving, fatherly response is still vital.

> *The last thing you want to convey now, even inadvertently, is that your love has melted away. So hide the awkwardness, Dad, and hug your daughter like you did when she was six!*

Just like their mothers, our daughters need to be hugged regularly, perhaps every day.

Knock Down Barriers,
BUILD BRIDGES

I want to share something neat that my dad did for me. When I was probably seven or eight, we were driving to the beach on a vacation. I was in the back of the car and had my feet on the console between the front seats. My dad was driving, and we were at a stoplight when he reached back and touched my foot. He said, 'You have the cutest feet.' It meant a lot to me because I was a dancer, and sometimes my feet were not that nice, but to this day I love my feet.

Just that simple compliment stayed with me.
It was as though my dad selected that one
feature to affirm. It still means so much to
me. I'll never forget it.

From a Female College Student

You might consider what that dad did to be an insignificant gesture, and yet his daughter remembered it vividly years later. It illustrates just how important kindness and compliments are to children, and especially to girls. Conversely, even mild criticism or ridicule, especially about the physical body, can be very hurtful to a sensitive individual.

Dads who want to connect with their little girls, and even those who are not so little, need to spend one-on-one time with them. It is an excellent way to knock down barriers and build bridges. Take your daughter somewhere she will like, such as out to breakfast or dinner. It doesn't have to be a big deal. Just make it a quiet time together when the two of you can sit and talk. Play miniature golf together, or check out a DVD at the library that the two of you can watch at home. If your daughter is younger, go to a kids' movie or a theme park.

Put these activities on the calendar, and do not let the

dates get canceled or postponed. Never leave kids wondering why you didn't show up and didn't even call. That can be more painful to a girl than not promising in the first place.

Once adolescence comes crashing on the scene, your teenager may be embarrassed to be seen with you. That's okay. Play by her rules, whatever they are.

Never forget that girls are made out of the same stuff their mothers are. Put sweet little notes and cards in your daughter's coat pocket or in her shoe. Write a short prayer and put it under her pillow. Girls love flowers. It's in their DNA! They beam when you express pride to others about them.

Look for anything that will bring your daughter into your world or you into hers. While you are at it, tell her you love her every time you are together.

You will be her hero forever.

Look for anything that will bring your daughter into your world or you into hers.

Give the Love Only You CAN GIVE

I n talking with many college-age women in the process of doing research for this book, the most frequent comment I heard was this:

> *My father is a good man. He has worked hard to earn a living for our family, and he's been faithful to my mother. Still, I never felt that he really admired or wanted to be close to me. He was very, very busy doing what he did, but he didn't have time for me. I felt like I was just there around the house, but he often didn't even seem to notice me.*

In response to hearing me say that, one girl said, "That describes exactly what I feel. And I've heard it from so many of my friends. In fact, our greatest uneasiness about getting married is the fear that our future husbands will not be affirming and caring. Another girl added, "It is essential that girls get affirmation from their fathers, because that's something I didn't experience growing up. That is the foundation of all my insecurities—the feeling that I wasn't really loved by my father. It is the root of everything I'm dealing with."

But another girl gave this beautiful expression of a dad who gave his daughter the love that only he could give her. This is an example well worth following:

> *I am blessed to have a father who spent time with*
> *me when I was growing up. Being the second of*
> *ten children, you might think my dad couldn't*
> *give me any special attention, and yet he spent*
> *a lot of time with us individually. He'd get up*
> *at five in the morning to take one of us out to*
> *breakfast for a couple of hours. He tried to do*
> *that with each child once a month. And then*
> *when I turned sixteen, he started taking me out*
> *to dinner instead. Those were times when he*

would ask what was going on in my life, and
then he would say, "Do you know how proud I
am of you? Do you know how much I love you?"
Those were the two questions he always asked as
we finished eating.

He had another ritual that, even though
it was a small thing, meant so much to me.
I depended on it every single night. He went
around to each of the kids' beds one at a time, and
he sat there and scratched our backs and hugged
us. And then he said the same prayer over us. He
did that throughout our childhoods. It was such a
special part of my growing up. I'll tell you, it was
very difficult for me when I was away at college
not to have him praying for me at bedtime.

He would say, "Heavenly Father, thank
You for a daughter like Sherrie. Thank You for
blessing her and putting her in this family. Thank
You for helping her find You at an early age.
Protect her tonight as she sleeps and tomorrow
as she goes through her day. Keep her from the
enemy and from harm. Help her to find a godly

*husband in Your time. In Jesus' name, amen." It
was always the same, every night.*

*That beautiful prayer will be with me for the
rest of my life. And I'll pray it over my kids too,
and I'll encourage my future husband to do it too.*

Why Dads Matter

When the chemistry is right, fathers make contributions to the welfare of their daughters in almost every dimension of life. Here is a quick overview of some related findings in that regard. After reading it, you'll see again why you matter as a dad to your daughter.

* *Girls whose fathers provide warmth and control achieve greater academic success.*[15]

* *Girls who are close to their fathers exhibit less anxiety and withdrawal behaviors.*[16]

* *Parental connectedness is the number one factor in preventing girls from engaging in premarital sex and indulging in drugs and alcohol.*[17]

❧ *Daughters who believe that their fathers care about them have significantly fewer suicide attempts and fewer instances of body dissatisfaction, depression, low self-esteem, substance abuse, and unhealthy weight.*[18]

❧ *Girls with involved fathers are twice as likely to stay in school.*[19]

❧ *Girls with fathers or father figures feel more protected, are more likely to attempt college, and are less likely to drop out of college.*[20]

❧ *Girls whose parents divorce or separate before they turn twenty-one tend to have shorter life spans by four years.*[21]

❧ *Girls with good fathers are less likely to seek male attention by flaunting themselves.*[22]

❧ *Girls who live with their mothers and fathers (as opposed to mothers only) have significantly fewer growth and developmental delays, and fewer learning disorders, emotional disabilities, and behavioral problems.*[23]

❧ *Girls who live with their mothers only have significantly less ability to control impulses and delay gratification, and have a weaker sense of conscience about right and wrong.*[24]

❧ *Both boys and girls do better academically if their fathers establish rules and exhibit affection.*[25]

When the chemistry is right, fathers make contributions to the welfare of their daughters in almost every dimension of life.

Does She Know She's YOUR PRINCESS?

Charm is deceptive, and beauty is fleeting,

but a woman who fears the Lord is to be praised.

Proverbs 31:30

The idea of Cinderella and other legendary princesses from the land of make-believe has captured the heart of almost every little girl today—including my daughter, Danae, who has loved the princess fantasy since she was a tiny girl. When I asked her why the story line is so captivating, she said: "To be a princess is to be considered beautiful, to be pursued, and to see all your hopes and dreams come true."

We can all understand why little girls want to join this happy club. I also believe that it gives expression to their inner yearning to love and be loved and live "happily ever after," as well as their quest for respect and dignity. The princess stories promote virtue, femininity, kindness, courtesy, work ethic, service to others, and "good vibes" about one's personhood. Where else in the popular culture—which includes an abundance of highly sexualized fashion and entertainment products marketed to girls—do you find these values represented in such an attractive way?

Yet not every little girl can always be the "fairest in the land" and look like Disney's Ariel or Sleeping Beauty. There is, therefore, an aspect to the princess fantasy that parents should recognize and respond to with wisdom and sensitivity. The worship of beauty is so pervasive that it influences every aspect of childhood. Our children will learn far more directly from us than from storybook fantasies.

Admittedly, life is not always a Cinderella journey, but let's let our little daughters be children while they are children.

Be There for Her

Very early in life, a child begins to learn the social importance of physical beauty. The values of society cannot be kept from little ears, and many adults do not even try to conceal their bias. Every child can figure out that the unattractive do not become "Miss America," nor do they become cheerleaders or movie stars.

What a distorted system of values we propagate! What irreparable damage is done to a struggling child whose parents do not intervene as allies. She can neither explain nor apologize. She can't even hide. Cruel voices follow her wherever she goes, whispering evil messages in her immature ears: "The other children don't like you." "See, I told you you'd fail." "You're different." "You're foolish." "They hate you." "You're worthless!" As time passes, the voices get louder and more urgent, until they obliterate all other sounds in an adolescent's mind.

Be there for your kids when the pressure is on. You hold the keys to their survival, and you must not be too busy to notice what is coming down. Teach them skills that will give them a sense of identity; treat them with dignity and respect, even when they fail to earn it at times; choose your words very carefully during periods of greatest sensitivity; and help them make friends by opening your home and your heart to lost kids looking for a safe place.

> *There are no magic answers, but there are good answers. Remember that this girl who is driving you crazy will someday be your best friend, if you handle her with care.*

My father told my sister and me that it was the inner beauty that mattered. He would also tell us how beautiful we were on the outside. And so that's what got me through junior high and high school, because I dealt with self-esteem issues. I'll never forget in sixth grade, having people ask me, 'Why don't you look like your sister?' I was a very late bloomer, but she was an early bloomer. So I had four years of extreme insecurity where people would say, 'Why are you shorter, and why are you so skinny? What's wrong with you?' My dad got me through that. If it weren't for him, I don't know what I would have done.

From a Female College Student

Discipline with
LOVE *and* RESPECT

As a father, you are going to confront contests of wills with your daughter many times. In those moments where your authority as a parent is challenged, it is extremely important for you to "win." Why? Because a child who behaves in ways that are disrespectful or harmful to herself or others often has a hidden motive. Whether she recognizes it or not, she is usually seeking to verify the existence and stability of the boundaries. A child who defies the leadership of her parents is reassured when they remain confident and firm under fire. It creates a sense of security for a kid who lives in a structured environment in which the rights of other people (and her own) are protected by well-defined limits.

With that said, here are the how-tos of shaping a child's will. I've boiled this complex topic down to six straightforward guidelines from my book *The New Strong-Willed Child* that I hope will be helpful, the first of which is most important. . . .

First: Begin Teaching Respect for Authority While Children Are Very Young

The most urgent advice I can give to the parents of an assertive, independent child is to establish their positions as strong but loving leaders when Missy is in the preschool years. This is the first step toward helping her learn to control her powerful impulses. Alas, there is no time to lose, because a naturally defiant youngster is in a high-risk category for antisocial behavior later in life. She is more likely to challenge her teachers in school and question the values she has been taught. Her temperament leads her to oppose anyone who tries to tell her what to do. Fortunately, this outcome is not inevitable, because the complexities of the human personality make it impossible to predict behavior with complete accuracy. But the probabilities lie in that direction. Thus, you must begin shaping the will of the particularly aggressive child very early in life. (Notice that I did not say to crush her will or to destroy it or to snuff it out, but to rein it in for her own good.) But how is that accomplished?

Well, first let me tell you how not to approach that objective. Harshness, gruffness, and sternness are not effective in shaping a child's will. Likewise, constant whacking and threatening and criticizing are destructive and counterproductive. A parent who is mean and angry most of the time is creating resentment that will be stored and come roaring into the relationship during adolescence or beyond. Therefore, every opportunity should be taken to keep the tenor of the home pleasant, fun, and accepting. At the same time, however, parents should display confident firmness in their demeanor. You, Dad, are the boss. You are in charge. If you believe it, your daughter will accept it also.

Second: Define the Boundaries before They Are Enforced

Preceding any disciplinary event is the necessity of establishing reasonable expectations and boundaries for the child. She should know what is and is not acceptable behavior before she is held responsible for it. This precondition will eliminate the sense of injustice that a youngster feels when she is punished or scolded for violating a vague or unidentified rule.

Third: Distinguish between Willful Defiance and Childish Irresponsibility

There is a world of difference between childish irresponsibility and "willful defiance." Understanding the distinction will be useful in knowing how to interpret the meaning of a behavior and how to respond to it appropriately. For instance, children regularly spill things, lose things, break things, forget things, and mess up things. That's the way kids are made. These behaviors represent the mechanism by which children are protected from adult-level cares and burdens. When accidents happen, patience and tolerance are the order of the day. If the foolishness was particularly pronounced for the age and maturity of the individual, you might want to have the youngster help with the cleanup or even work to pay for the loss. Otherwise, I think the event should be ignored.

There is another category of behavior, however, that is strikingly different. It occurs when a child blatantly defies the authority of the parent. She may shout "I will not!" or "You shut up!" or "You can't make me." It may happen when she throws a violent temper tantrum in order to get her way. These behaviors represent a willful, haughty spirit and a determination to disobey. Something very different is going on in those moments. You have drawn a line in the dirt, and she has deliberately stepped across it. You're both asking, "Who is going to win? Who is in charge here?" If you do not conclusively answer these questions for her, she will precipitate other battles designed to ask them again and again.

Fourth: Reassure and Teach after the Confrontation Is Over

After a time of conflict during which you have demonstrated your right to lead (particularly if it resulted in tears for the child), the youngster between two and seven (or older) will probably want to be loved and reassured. By all means, open your arms and let her come! Hold her close and tell her of your love. Rock her gently and let her know again why she was punished and how she can avoid the trouble next time. This is a teachable moment, when the objective of your discipline can be explained. And for the Christian family, it is extremely important to pray with the child at that time, admitting to God that we have all sinned and no one is perfect. Divine forgiveness is a marvelous experience, even for a very young child.

Fifth: Avoid Impossible Demands

Be absolutely sure that your child is capable of delivering what you require. Never punish her for wetting the bed involuntarily or for not becoming potty trained by one year of age or for doing poorly in school when she is incapable of academic success. These impossible demands put the child in an irresolvable conflict: there is no way out. That condition brings unnecessary risks to the human emotional apparatus. Besides that, it is simply unjust.

Sixth: Let Love Be Your Guide!

A relationship that is characterized by genuine love and affection is likely to be a healthy one, even though some parental mistakes and errors are inevitable. These six steps should form the foundation for healthy parent-child relationships.[26]

A relationship that is
characterized by genuine love
and affection is likely to
be a healthy one.

Win the Battle
OF WILLS

It is not unusual, especially after reaching puberty, for daughters to exhibit disrespectful teen attitudes, especially ranting and raving in angry outbursts. In these situations, you must be the father, and lead like one. You hold the keys to everything your little girl wants and needs: permission to do things, transportation, allowances (if any), coveted clothing, provision of meals, ironing and laundry, and access to television and computer. It is all under your supervision; or at least, it should be. I suggest that you have a little talk with her and tell her that you know she is going through a tough time but that she has to work harder at controlling her anger. It is not helping her, and it is hurting the rest of the family. This is why you are going to help her be more civil. From now on, everything that she wants will depend on her cooperation.

In the conversation you have with your daughter, say something like this: "I want you to know several things. First, I love you more than you will ever know. I brought you into the world, and I would lay down my life for you if necessary. Second, because I love you so much, I can't allow you to continue to act in a way that is harmful to you and to the rest of the family. It is going to stop right now. Third, I have an obligation before God to make you respectful to me and your mother first and then to your brothers and sisters. If you don't do it, I have many ways to make you miserable, and believe me when I say I will use every one of them.

"You have chosen to be very difficult, and until you decide to cooperate, this is not going to be a pleasant place for you. When you are tired of having no privileges and being cooped up here at home, we will determine where we go from there. Until then, it would be in your best interest to play by the rules, because they are going to be enforced. If you ever want to talk to me, I would be happy to hear your heart on things that you think are unfair or frustrating. But it will be unacceptable to scream, slam doors, and [fill in the blank]. Get it? Got it. Now, is there anything you want to say?"

Then have the courage to dole out those privileges and consequences with consistency and determination. Do not try to control your daughter with anger. It doesn't work. She not only doesn't care if you get mad—she has also won a strategic battle when you do. In short, you need to be far tougher than you have ever been, but not by acting like an out-of-control teenager. When she is ready to negotiate, respond with respect and firmness.

This battle you are in is
not one you can afford to lose.
You can win it!
God be with you!

Friends and Bullies

One mother told me that her daughter awakens early each morning before school and lies in bed wondering, *How can I get through this day without being humiliated?* She worries about not having someone to sit with at lunch and how to do her hair and select clothes in ways that will not bring her ridicule. Teens and adolescents are expected to wear not just any designer brands but the "right" ones. A mistake at this point can be catastrophic. For this girl and millions of others, school is a minefield through which they walk every day. A bomb could go off underneath them at any moment. Girls whose weight is normal are called "fat," and those who have unusual physical characteristics are mocked unmercifully. They are given nicknames to highlight the features they most want to hide.

Your daughter is likely to be impacted emotionally by bullying at some time during her developmental journey. "Friends and enemies" will be the key to everything for your daughter in the middle school years and beyond. Remember that her brain was wired for intimacy with others during infancy, and now in puberty she yearns for close relationships with her peers. Intimacy is the air she breathes and her reason for living. Study after study has demonstrated that human beings are social creatures and thrive better when they are loved and appreciated, even by a few people. Human beings desperately need the affirmation and support of one another at every stage of their lives. It is the way we were designed. The Creator gave us an innate longing for human friendship and affection, and then told us to meet those needs for one another.

> *When Jesus was asked by a teacher of the*
> *law which of the commandments was most*
> *important, He replied, "The most important one*
> *. . . is this: . . . 'Love the Lord your God with*
> *all your heart and with all your soul and with*
> *all your mind and with all your strength.' The*
> *second is this: 'Love your neighbor as yourself.'*
> *There is no commandment greater than these."*
>
> *Mark 12:29-31*

That's why when adolescent friendships go sour and rejection settles in, emotional crises are inevitable for the girl who has been thrown overboard. To her, the parting can seem like the end of the world. Two girls may have grown up together and spent countless hours sharing their most intimate feelings and fears. Trust was once the hallmark of their relationship. Then suddenly the rejected girl is treated like the scum of the earth. Her former best buddy won't return text messages or phone calls. Barbed humor is used to embarrass and humiliate the rejected girl in front of others. No one wants to sit with her at lunch or at a ball game for fear of alienating the more powerful girl. The rejected girl may have no idea why it has happened, and indeed, there might have been no precipitating event—at least not a visible one. Without warning or explanation, she appears to be hated by the girl who matters to her most.

This is what many girls are dealing with today. What can be done to help them?

Many authorities on the prevention of bullying emphasize the importance of talking to children and teens about what they are experiencing. Dr. Cheryl Dellasega says, "Support your daughter: If she comes home talking about a specific incident, help her explore the details and her emotions, [and] look for alternative ways to respond and practice what she will do next time."[27]

At the core of these strategies is the importance of parents talking with their children and teens. That can be difficult to do. Many kids don't want the involvement of their parents for fear of making matters worse. "Leave me alone" is their typical response. There is nothing more humiliating than for moms and dads to interject themselves into peer relationships. Some of these bullied teens may take out their anger and frustration on Mom and Dad, who have done nothing to deserve the abuse to which they are subjected. At the root of it all is embarrassment at home and at school.

Regardless of the method you choose,
the more you can demonstrate to your daughter
that you care and are on her team,
the better the outcome.

The most important suggestion I have to offer to parents of daughters who are in the midst of the storm is this: *There might come a time to get your daughter out of it.* You have to be prepared to do whatever is necessary to preserve her tender spirit. If you realize your daughter has lost the battle against the taunters and harassers, she needs you to intervene. It might make sense to sit down with her and talk about a change of schools. In some cases, a child can completely recalibrate socially in a new setting with an increased level of confidence. Perhaps there is a Christian school nearby that would be affordable and consistent with your beliefs. Maybe a private school would be appropriate. Another option for you might be homeschooling, which can be a wonderful alternative for the immature child in the early grades who is not able to cope socially.

The point is that you can't just sit idly by and watch your child go down for the count. When I was sixteen years old, my parents moved us seven hundred miles away to give me a new start. I corrected some mistakes, learned some new lessons, and made a large number of new friends. Everything changed for me during my last two years of high school. My mom and dad cared enough about me to help me land on my feet.

Do not just sit by and watch your daughter go down for the count.

Your Most Significant RESPONSIBILITY

"Am I lovely? Am I worth fighting for? Have
I been and will I continue to be romanced?"
When these questions are answered, Yes, a
restful, quiet spirit settles in a woman's heart.

And every woman can have these questions
answered, Yes. You have been and you will
continue to be romanced all your life. Yes. Our
God finds you lovely. Jesus has moved heaven
and earth to win you for himself. He will not
rest until you are completely his.[28]

John and Stasi Eldredge

These words from the Eldredges are inspiring and entirely accurate. There is within the nature of girls a yearning to know that they are precious to someone who loves them wholeheartedly. While boys are fantasizing about conquest and heroic deeds, little girls are already dreaming about the arrival of a Prince Charming who will sweep them off their feet. They hope to marry and live together in a little love nest made just for two. But as we know, life does not always deliver on that promise. The prince sometimes turns out to be fickle or flawed, or he may never show up at all.

Even if their storybook marriage becomes a reality, as it has for Shirley and me and millions of others, women often experience a longing for something more. That *something* is not romantic in nature. It is a hunger for a relationship with the compassionate and caring God, whose love is constant and secure. He never disappoints or forgets. He is there in times of loss and sorrow, and He hears the faintest cry. As King David wrote, "The LORD is a refuge for the oppressed, a stronghold in times of trouble" (Psalm 9:9). David also said, "The LORD is close to the brokenhearted and saves those who are crushed in spirit" (Psalm 34:18). Every child, male and female, should become intimately acquainted with this Friend and Savior during his or her developmental years.

If it is true that children should be trained in the knowledge of the Lord, and Scripture tells us it is, then there is one task in parenting that outranks all others in significance. *It is the responsibility of Christian mothers and fathers to introduce their children to Jesus Christ and to cultivate their understanding of Him at every opportunity.* The apostle Paul gave us that priority two thousand years ago when he wrote Ephesians 6:4:

Do not exasperate
your children;
instead, bring them
up in the training
and instruction of the Lord.

Teach Your Daughter Well

These commandments that I give you today are to be upon your hearts. Impress them on your children. Talk about them when you sit at home and when you walk along the road, when you lie down and when you get up. Tie them as symbols on your hands and bind them on your foreheads. Write them on the doorframes of your houses and on your gates.

Deuteronomy 6:6-9

Moses didn't just make a "suggestion" to parents about the spiritual training of their children. He called that assignment a commandment. Talk to your children about the Lord and His mercies continually. This is what Moses told the children of Israel. It is also what King David and the prophet Joel, among other biblical authors, instructed us to do (Psalm 34:11; 78:4, 6; 145:4; Joel 1:3). These passages are too clear to be misunderstood.

Take advantage of every opportunity to tell your children that faith in God is extremely important and that He cares about them too. Begin this introduction to spiritual truths when your children are very young. Even at three years of age, a child is capable of learning that the flowers, the sky, the birds, and even rainbows are gifts from God's hand. He made these wonderful things, just as He created each one of us. The first Scripture our children should learn is, "God is love" (1 John 4:8). They should be taught to thank Him before eating their food and to ask for His help when they are hurt or scared.

In a 2003 nationwide poll, researcher George Barna observed that children ages five through thirteen have a 32 percent probability of accepting Christ as their Savior. That rate drops dramatically to just 4 percent for kids ages fourteen through eighteen. And those who have not become Christians before age nineteen have only a 6 percent probability of doing so during the rest of their lives. [29]

There is no time to lose!

Give Her the Divine Source of Wisdom

Thy word have I hid in mine heart,

that I might not sin against thee.

Psalm 119:11, KJV

If you want your daughter to be guided morally when she is beyond your reach and after she is grown, you should begin teaching favorite Bible passages to her when she is young. It is amazing how often a relevant biblical reference zings to the surface just when a situation comes up that requires wisdom and discernment. If those verses have not been "downloaded" to our brains, we will have to figure out what to do based on our own limited understanding.

Memorize key Scriptures with her, make a game out of the process, and reward her for learning these passages. Some of the stored passages will stay with her for a lifetime, and even if the exact words are forgotten, the truths they contain remain alive and will be remembered.

Music is a wonderful tool for teaching the Scriptures. Introduce your daughter to an array of songs that contain biblical concepts and stories. You can begin with "Jesus loves me, this I know, for the Bible tells me so." Being a traditionalist myself, I prefer songs that have endured for many years. You may prefer more contemporary music, of course, but just be sure that your daughter grows up with the lyrics and stories of the Christian faith. Then get her into a strong church that preaches the Word of God and will help you bring her up in the training and instruction of the Lord.

If you want your daughter to be guided morally after she is grown, begin teaching favorite Bible passages to her when she is young.

The Power OF PRAYER

Pray without ceasing.

1 Thessalonians 5:17, KJV

Begin teaching your children to pray as early as possible. Prayer is one of God's most mysterious and remarkable gifts to us. It is our lifeline to heaven, our lifeline to the most holy of relationships, our opportunity to directly express our praises and desires to the Creator of the universe. There is power in this simple act that cannot fully be explained, yet can never be denied. And it is our most effective means of contributing to the welfare of our children.

You may be aware that my wife, Shirley, is chairman of the National Day of Prayer Task Force. Prayer has been the passion of her life, beginning at six years of age when she gave her heart to the Lord. This is her message to moms and dads:

When [our daughter] Danae was about three years old, Jim and I realized that as parents we needed divine help. We began fasting and praying for her, and later for [our son] Ryan almost every week (a practice that I continue to this day).

Our prayer went something like this: "Lord, give us the wisdom to raise the precious children You have loaned to us, and above all else, help us bring them to the feet of Jesus. This is more important to us than our health or our work or our finances. What we ask most fervently is that the circle be unbroken when we meet in heaven."

God has not only heard this prayer but blessed it in ways we never anticipated. Our prayer time has become a project that Jim and I enjoy *together*, drawing us closer to each other as we draw closer to God. In addition, the act of fasting each week serves as an important reminder of our priorities: It's difficult to forget your highest values when one day out of seven is spent focusing entirely on them. Finally, our children were influenced by these acts of discipline. When they observed us fasting or praying, it gave us the opportunity to explain why we did these things, how much we loved them, and how much we loved and trusted the Lord.

God hears and honors—in His perfect timing—our petitions on behalf of our children. If you want the very best for your sons and daughters, I urge you to call on the greatest power in the universe in frequent prayer.[30]

Are you praying with your little ones? How about your older children? Don't let the golden opportunities slip away.

The warmest memory of all from my childhood, and what shaped my life, was waking up very early in the morning and seeing a small light on in another room. It might have been five o'clock or even four. I would get up and find my dad sitting in his chair and holding a cup of coffee. He would be reading the Bible. I would come up beside him and say, "Good morning, Dad." And he would put his arm around me and say, "This is what I just read, Robin. I just prayed this verse for you." And he would put my name beside it in his Bible, and he would pray over me.

From a Female College Student

Pray without ceasing.

[113]

She Is Worth THE SACRIFICE

Good parenting almost always requires sacrifice.

Let me acknowledge that successful family life is difficult to achieve. It is never perfect and is often problematic. I am sure you have your own set of challenges as you seek to meet the needs of your children. You may be a single parent with very limited financial resources. Perhaps you suffer from illness, disability, or addiction. Or maybe you have strong-willed kids who are tough to handle. The last thing I want to do is add to your pressures or sense of frustration. Nevertheless, *if there is any way you can give priority to your children amid those limitations, even if it requires serious sacrifice, you will not regret giving it to them.*

This might mean staying married when your impulse is to divorce. It could cause you to make choices that will handicap you professionally. It might mean financial hardship for the family because Mom is staying at home with her children. It might mean giving up your four-hour golf outing every Saturday. What I am saying is that from where I sit today, children are worth everything they cost us.

It was this perspective that led me to walk away from my position as a professor of pediatrics at the University of Southern California School of Medicine. Honestly, I thought I was walking away from the good life when I left academia. But as the years unfolded, I realized that I hadn't actually given up

Children are worth everything
they cost us.

much of anything. I just found other ways to use my training and opportunities, and I was more fulfilled than I had been in my "other life." I thank God now that my father urged me to give priority to my family. The wonderful relationship I enjoy with our grown son and daughter today is the payoff.

I hope you will find a way to give your little girls (and boys) the great benefits of a secure, loving home. That is the surest way to preserve the light that shines in their eyes.

Every Dad
Has Some Regrets

We can no more be perfect parents than we can be perfect human beings. The task of raising kids in a fast-paced world is infinitely complex, and life itself takes a toll on our good intentions. But kids are resilient, and they usually manage to turn out rather well.

Remember that the Creator in the Garden of Eden also had "children" who were rebellious. In that instance, Adam and Eve had no television, pornography, bad peers, or other unsavory influences to lead them astray. And yet they were headstrong and went their own way. It is the nature of mankind. What I am saying is that it would be a mistake for you to wallow in guilt for everything your children do wrong.

Kids are exposed to many harmful influences today. It is impossible to shield them from everything negative. We do the best we can to guide them down today's River of Culture and try to keep them from drowning.

> *To blame yourself for everything disappointing*
> *that you see in your children is not biblical,*
> *not reasonable, and not fair.*

On the other hand, it is inappropriate for parents to take the credit for everything good in their children. Each individual is a free moral agent who is able to make independent decisions. Some of those choices turn out to be good and others bad, but you are not to blame for them all.

Ezekiel 18:2–4 says: "What do you people mean by quoting this proverb about the land of Israel: 'The fathers eat sour grapes, and the children's teeth are set on edge'? As surely as I live, declares the Sovereign Lᴏʀᴅ, you will no longer quote this proverb in Israel. For every living soul belongs to me, the father as well as the son—both alike belong to me. The soul who sins is the one who will die."

What this Scripture is telling us is that there is no such

Your job now is to pray earnestly
for the spiritual welfare
of your children.

thing as "generational sin." Each person is responsible for his or her own choices and behavior. Parents can try to teach moral principles to their children, but ultimately the accountability passes to the progeny.

As a dad, whatever you did right or wrong in the past is done. That record is in the books. Lay it to rest. Ask the Lord to override your shortcomings and failings, and to work to accomplish His purposes in their hearts and lives. Your job now is to pray earnestly for the spiritual welfare of your children. Continue to show love to them, and when your advice is asked for, give it thoughtfully. But do not let the demon of guilt ride heavy on your shoulders. That is a short route to despair.

Remember, Dads

Be the leader of your family by setting boundaries.

Shower your daughter with small gestures of kindness.

Build your daughter up with compliments rather than consistently pointing out her flaws.

Stay connected with your daughter even if you have disappointed or failed her in some way.

Never stop asking your daughter questions about what's going on in her life.

Love your daughter. If she knows her earthly father loves her, it will be easier for her to understand and accept her heavenly Father's love.

Pray with your daughter as often as you can, and when you are away from each other, hold her in your prayers with your wife.

You may notice I have given you seven tips—one for each day in the week. Why not make it your goal this week to try them all? Please do not be discouraged if you are not in the habit of doing some of them. It may feel awkward at first if your daughter shrugs off a compliment or claims she's "too old" for a hug. I assure you that in her heart she will notice that you are reaching out to her.

Keep looking for opportunities to demonstrate your love and commitment.
With God's help, you will recognize them.

May He bless this precious daughter He has loaned to you for a brief season.

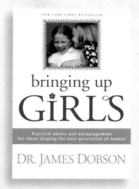

Endnotes

1 Margaret J. Meeker, *Strong Fathers, Strong Daughters: 10 Secrets Every Father Should Know* (New York: Ballantine Books, 2006), 8–9, 18, 28.

2 Tanya S. Scheffler and Peter J. Naus, "The Relationship between Fatherly Affirmation and a Woman's Self-Esteem, Fear of Intimacy, Comfort with Womanhood and Comfort with Sexuality," *Canadian Journal of Human Sexuality* 8, no. 1 (Spring 1999): 39–45; Meeker, *Strong Fathers, Strong Daughters.*

3 Meeker, *Strong Fathers, Strong Daughters*, 28.

4 Alan Ebert, "Oprah Winfrey Talks Openly about Oprah," *Good Housekeeping*, September 1991, 63.

5 John and Stasi Eldredge, *Captivating: Unveiling the Mystery of a Woman's Soul* (Nashville: Thomas Nelson, 2005), 46, 59.

6 Michael Gurian, Ph.D., *The Wonder of Girls* (New York: Simon and Schuster, 2002), 53.

7 Allan Pease and Allan Garner, *Talk Language: How to Use Conversation for Profit and Pleasure* (London: Simon and Schuster, 1985).

8 Quoted in E. D. Hill, *I'm Not Your Friend, I'm Your Parent: Helping Your Children Set the Boundaries They Need . . . and Really Want* (Nashville: Thomas Nelson Publishers, 2008), 16.

9 Gurian, *The Wonder of Girls*, 75.

10 Louann Brizendine, *The Female Brain* (New York: Morgan Road Books, 2006), 13.

11 I. F. Bielsky and L. J. Young, "Oxytocin, Vasopressin, and Social Recognition and Reduction in Anxiety-Like Behavior in Vasopressin V1a Receptor Knockout Mice," *Neuropsychopharmacology* 29, no. 3 (2004): 483–493; C. S. Carter, "Developmental Consequences of Oxytocin," *Physiology and Behavior* 79, no. 3 (2003): 383–397.

12 Ibid.

13 Brizendine, *The Female Brain*, 58.

14 Meeker, *Strong Fathers, Strong Daughters*, 96; Debra Haffner, *Beyond the Big Talk: A Parent's Guide to Raising Sexually Healthy Teens—from Middle School to High School and Beyond* (New York: Newmarket Press, 2001).

15 Rebekah Coley, "Children's Socialization Experiences and Functioning in Single-Mother Households: The Importance of Fathers and Other Men," *Child Development* 69 (February 1998): 219–230.

16 A. Morcoen and K. Verschuren, "Representation of Self and Socioemotional Competence in Kindergartners: Differential and Combined Effects of Attachment to Mothers and Fathers," *Child Development* 70 (1999): 183–201.

17 Michael D. Resnick et al., *Journal of the American Medical Association* 10 (September 10, 1997): 823-832.

18 Diann Ackard et al., *American Journal of Preventive Medicine* 1 (January 30, 2006): 59–66.

19 U.S. Department of Health and Human Services, National Center for Health Statistics, "Survey on Child Health" (Washington, D.C.: GPO, 1993).

20 Greg J. Duncan, Martha Hill, and W. Jean Yeung, "Fathers' Activities and Children's Attainments" (paper presented at a conference on father involvement, Washington, D.C.).

21 Joseph E. Schwartz et al., "Sociodemographic and Psychosocial Factors in Child as Predictors of Adult Mortality," *American Journal of Public Health* 85 (1995): 1237–1245.

22 Claudette Wassil-Grimm, *Where's Daddy? How Divorced, Single and Widowed Mothers Can Provide What's Missing When Dad's Missing* (New York: Overlook Press, 1994).

23 N. Zill and Carol Schoenborn, "Child Development, Learning and Emotional Problems: Health of Our Nation's Children," U.S. Department of Health and Human Services, National Center for Health Statistics, Advance Data 1990 (Washington, D.C.: GPO, 1990).

24 E. M. Hetherington and Barbara Martin, "Family Interaction," *Psychopathological Disorders of Childhood* (New York: Wiley, 1979).

25 F. Horn and Tom Sylvester, *Father Facts* (Gaithersburg, MD: National Fatherhood Initiative, 2002).

26 James C. Dobson, *The New Strong-Willed Child* (Carol Stream, IL: Tyndale House Publishers, 2004), chapter 4.

27 Helena Oliviero, "Bully Girls: Intimidating Practices Grow among Female Teens," *Atlanta Journal-Constitution* (August 26, 2004): B1.

28 Eldredge, *Captivating*, 146.

29 John W. Kennedy, "The 4–14 Window," *Christianity Today* (July 2004), http://www.christianitytoday.com/ct/2004/july/37.53.html.

30 James and Shirley Dobson, *Night Light for Parents* (Carol Stream, IL: Tyndale House Publishers, 2002), 22.